First published 2008 by Walker Books Ltd
87 Vauxhall Walk, London SE11 5HJ

This edition published 2009

10 9 8 7 6 5 4 3 2 1

The right of Geoff Waring to be identified
as author/illustrator of this work has been
asserted by him in accordance with the
Copyright, Designs and Patents Act 1988

This book has been typeset in ITC Kabel

Printed in China

British Library Cataloguing in Publication Data:
a catalogue record for this book is available
from the British Library

ISBN: 978-1-4063-1868-5

For Sam, Steph, Paul, Lucy, Martin, Sue and Helen

The author and publisher would like to thank Sue Ellis
at the Centre for Literacy in Primary Education and
Martin Jenkins for their invaluable input and guidance
during the making of this book.

OSCAR and the BIRD

A BOOK ABOUT ELECTRICITY

Geoff Waring

WALKER BOOKS
AND SUBSIDIARIES
LONDON · BOSTON · SYDNEY · AUCKLAND

One day, Oscar saw a tractor standing in the field. He climbed up to look in the cab, when suddenly the windscreen wiper started to move …

swish, swish!

"How did that happen?"
Oscar wondered.

Bird flew down from her branch.
"Electricity is making the wiper move,"
she said. "You must have pressed
the switch by mistake."
"What's electricity?" Oscar asked.
"It's a kind of energy that people use to help
things move or make sounds,
or light up or heat up," Bird said.

"Where does it come from?"
Oscar wanted to know.
Bird hopped down to show
him the engine. "It flows
through wires from this battery,"
she said. "The battery has
chemicals inside it that make
electricity."
"It's a very big battery!" Oscar said.

"It's a big battery for a big tractor," Bird said. "Batteries come in all shapes and sizes – even a tiny one can make electricity."

And she told Oscar about some other machines that are powered by batteries...

Together, these two small batteries can make a strong light shine from a torch.

This rechargeable battery has powerful chemicals inside it that can make electricity strong enough to move a toy.

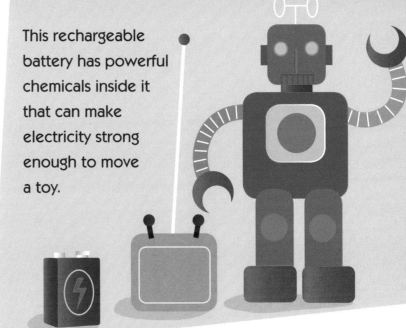

This tiny round battery can keep a watch ticking for more than two years.

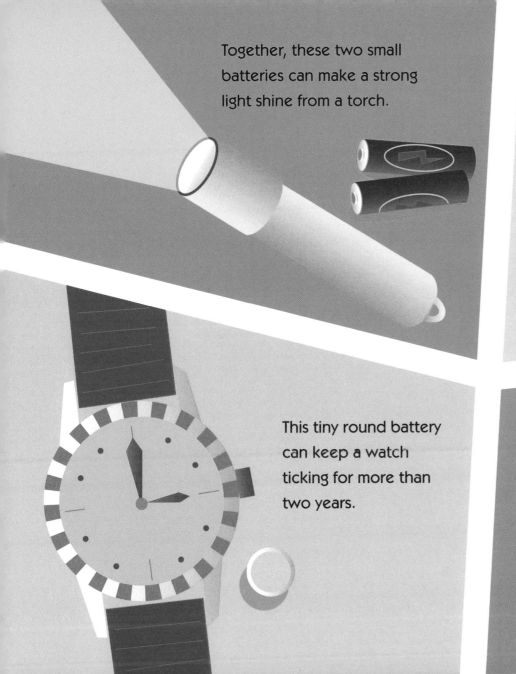

This long slim battery is powerful too, and light – just right for machines you carry around and use a lot.

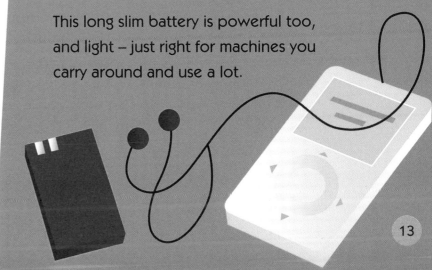

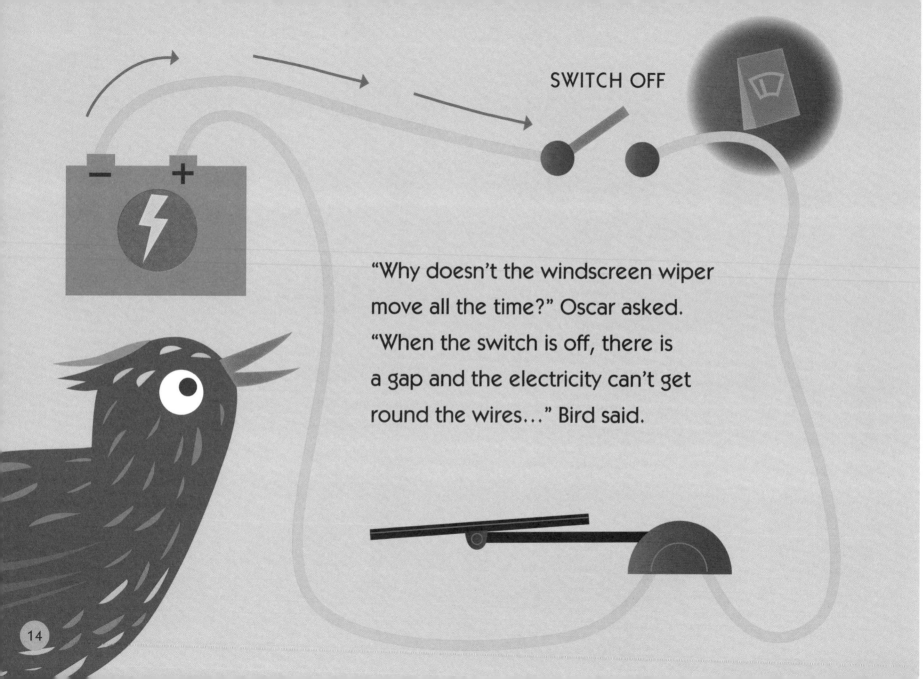

SWITCH OFF

"Why doesn't the windscreen wiper move all the time?" Oscar asked. "When the switch is off, there is a gap and the electricity can't get round the wires..." Bird said.

14

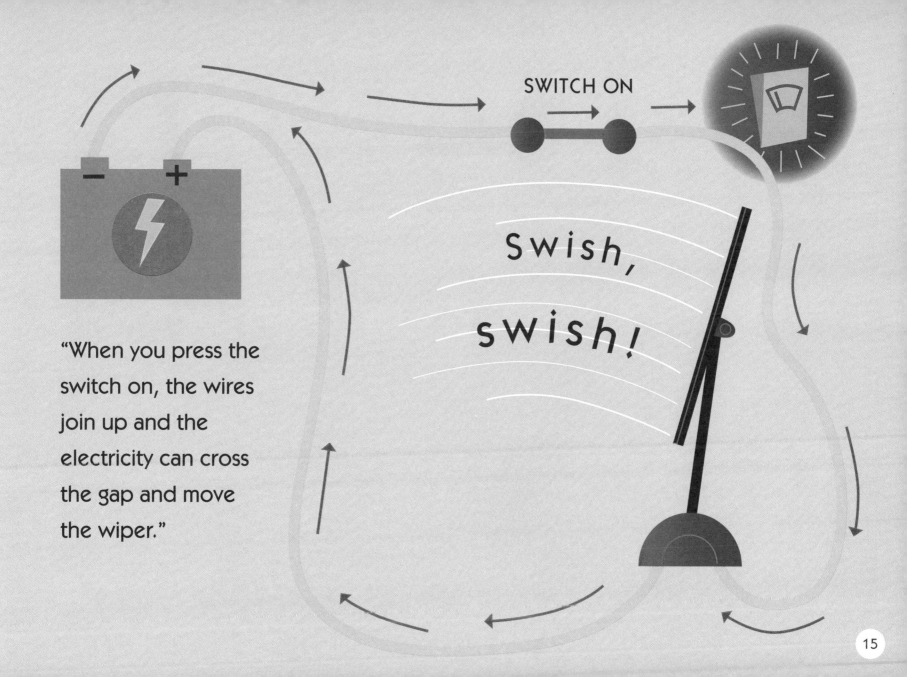

SWITCH ON

Swish,

swish!

"When you press the switch on, the wires join up and the electricity can cross the gap and move the wiper."

15

"Does everything in the tractor need electricity to work?" Oscar asked.

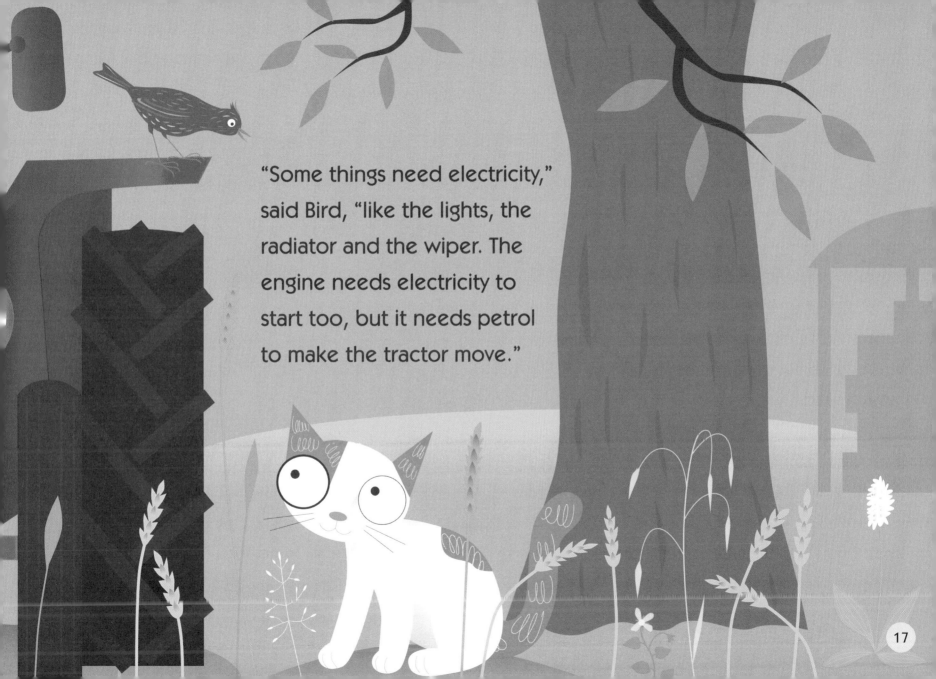

"Some things need electricity," said Bird, "like the lights, the radiator and the wiper. The engine needs electricity to start too, but it needs petrol to make the tractor move."

Oscar looked up. "Does electricity flow through those wires as well?" he asked Bird.
"Yes," Bird answered.

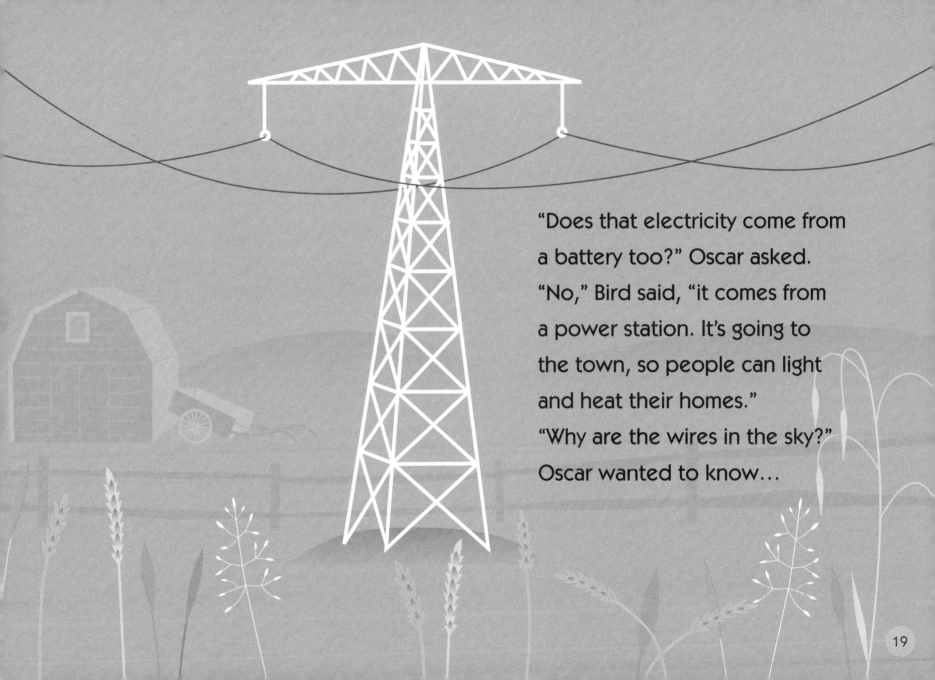

"Does that electricity come from a battery too?" Oscar asked. "No," Bird said, "it comes from a power station. It's going to the town, so people can light and heat their homes."
"Why are the wires in the sky?" Oscar wanted to know...

"So they're out of reach and you'll be safer!" Bird said. "They carry LOTS of electricity – and it would be very dangerous if it flowed through you. You should never touch a bare wire, Oscar."

Just then, in the distance,
they could see flashes of lightning.
"Lightning is electricity too," Bird said.
"There is a kind of electricity that's all around us,
but most of the time we don't see or notice it."

Over on the hill, the blades on the
wind turbines were turning in the wind.
"Is the electricity that's all around us helping them to move?" Oscar asked.
"It's the other way round!" Bird said. "The wind
turns the blades and the movement makes electricity."

Then it started to rain...
Oscar and Bird rushed
back to the tractor.

Swoosh, swoosh!

"The wiper is wiping the water away,
so we can see out," Bird said.
"Then let's not switch it off yet!" Oscar said.

27

Thinking some more about electricity

In the fields, Oscar found out about these things...

What electricity is for

Electricity is energy we use as power
to help us do things:

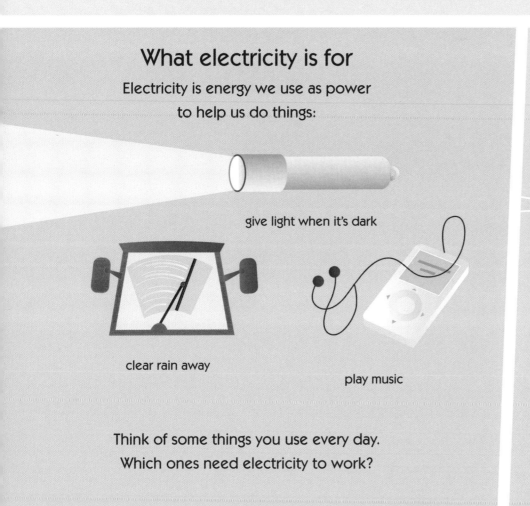

give light when it's dark

clear rain away

play music

Think of some things you use every day.
Which ones need electricity to work?

How electricity works

Electricity flows through wires. The wires are
made of metal to help the electricity flow easily.
Switches can stop or start the flow.

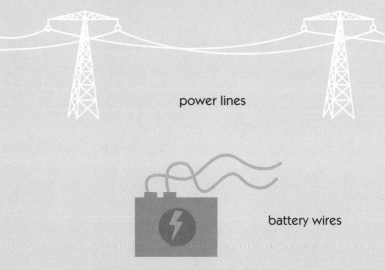

power lines

battery wires

Some electricity is so powerful, it's dangerous.
You must always be careful near wires and
batteries, plugs and sockets.

What electricity is made from

Electricity is made in different ways:

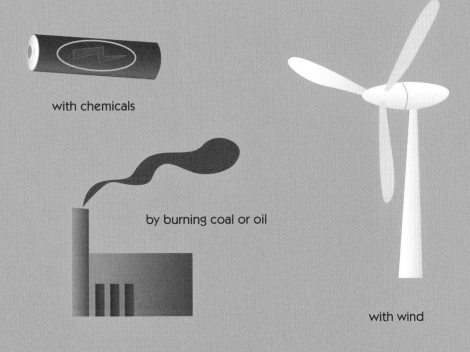

with chemicals

by burning coal or oil

with wind

There is always electricity around us too.

Oscar thinks electricity's great! Do you too?

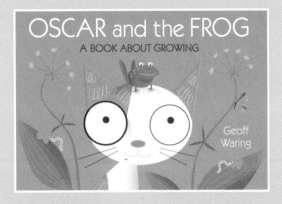

OSCAR and the FROG
A BOOK ABOUT GROWING
Geoff Waring

OSCAR and the MOTH
A BOOK ABOUT
LIGHT AND DARK
Geoff Waring

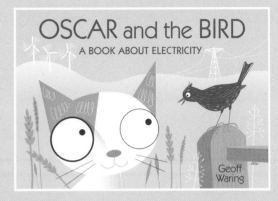

OSCAR and the BIRD
A BOOK ABOUT ELECTRICITY
Geoff Waring

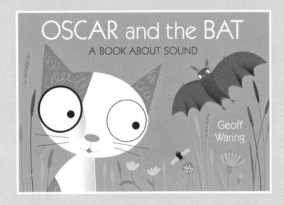

OSCAR and the BAT
A BOOK ABOUT SOUND
Geoff Waring

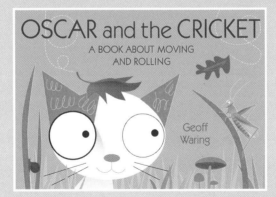

OSCAR and the CRICKET
A BOOK ABOUT MOVING
AND ROLLING
Geoff Waring

OSCAR and the SNAIL
A BOOK ABOUT THINGS WE USE
Geoff Waring

Which of these Oscar books have you read?